W9-CFB-104

Do You Know the Continents?

Learning about South America

Thomas K. Adamson

Lerner Publications ◆ Minneapolis

Content Consultant: Jose Javier Lopez, PhD, Professor of Geography, Minnesota State University

Lerner Publications Company
A division of Lerner Publishing Group, Inc.
241 First Avenue North
Minneapolis, MN 55401 USA

For reading levels and more information, look up this title at www.lernerbooks.com.

Library of Congress Cataloging-in-Publication Data

Adamson, Thomas K., 1970-
Learning about South America / by Thomas K. Adamson.
pages cm. — (Searchlight books. Do you know the continents?)
Includes index.
Audience: Grades 4 to 6.
ISBN 978-1-4677-8021-6 (lb : alk. paper) — ISBN 978-1-4677-8355-2 (pb : alk. paper) — ISBN 978-1-4677-8356-9 (eb pdf)
1. South America—Juvenile literature. I. Title.
F2208.5.A33 2015
980—dc23 2015000564

Manufactured in the United States of America
1 – VP – 7/15/15

Contents

Chapter 1

LAND OF WONDERS

South America is a continent of extremes. It has the world's longest mountain chain. It also has the world's largest rain forest. The world's second-longest river flows through South America. The continent is also home to Earth's highest waterfall. One of the world's driest deserts lies in South America too.

South America has busy cities and amazing landscapes. What is one record-holding feature you can see in South America?

South America is mostly in the Southern Hemisphere. The equator runs through its northern areas. The continent's northern edge connects to Central America. Its southern tip points toward Antarctica.

A statue marks the equator in the South American country of Ecuador.

SOUTH AMERICA SHARES A LAND BORDER WITH JUST ONE OTHER CONTINENT, NORTH AMERICA.

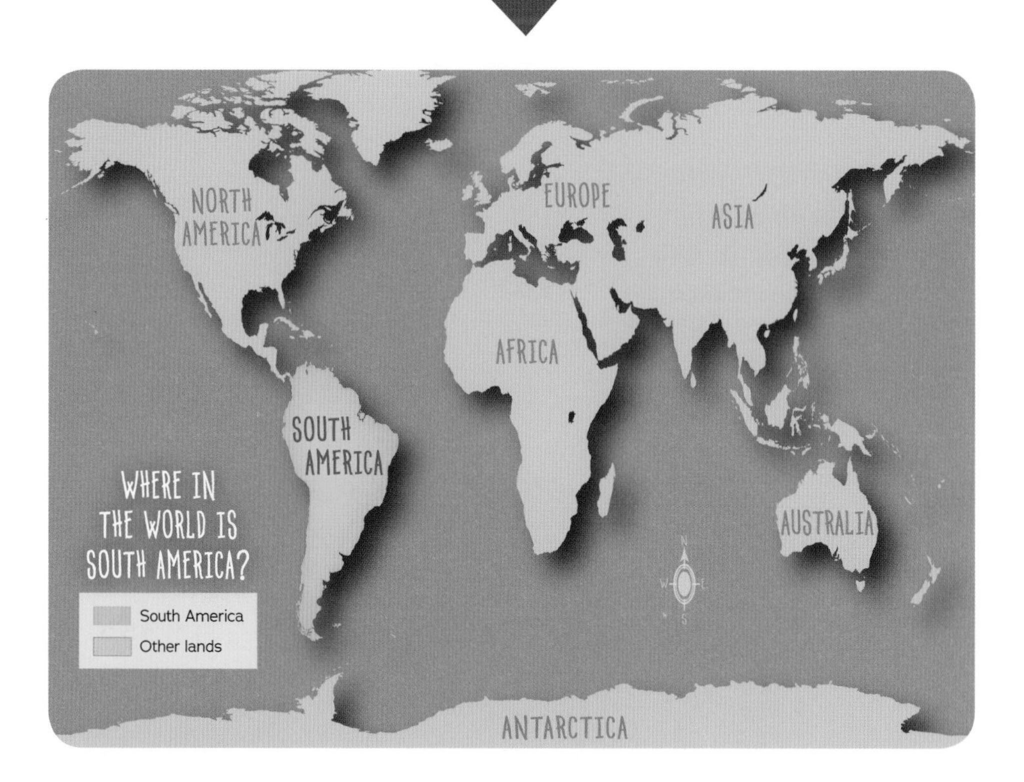

Booming Culture

South America is home to diverse cultures. Unique styles of music are found there. Cumbia and tango are among the most popular. Cumbia combines African and Spanish influences. It uses drums, maracas, and brass instruments. Tango often features two or more guitarists. People perform lively dances to tango music.

South Americans also enjoy sports. By far the most popular is soccer. South Americans call it football. People go wild for their favorite teams. Buenos Aires, the capital of Argentina, has more than ten teams all by itself! Whether you like landscapes, diverse cultures, or sports, there's something for everyone in South America!

Millions of kids in South America love to play soccer.

Chapter 2

COUNTRIES AND CITIES

Indigenous peoples have lived in South America for thousands of years. Europeans first arrived in the early 1500s. Spain and Portugal set up colonies. They took over the indigenous peoples' lands and brought slaves from Africa to work on their farms. The Dutch, French, and British also built colonies.

Before Europeans arrived, South American cultures had built large stone cities and temples. When did Europeans reach the continent?

Colonists resisted European rule in the early 1800s. Many of them formed new countries. They fought wars to win their independence.

MILITARY LEADER SIMÓN BOLÍVAR HELPED MANY NATIONS WIN THEIR INDEPENDENCE. THE COUNTRY OF BOLIVIA IS NAMED AFTER HIM.

La Boca is a popular tourist site in Buenos Aires.

Argentina

Argentina is the largest Spanish-speaking country in South America. One-third of Argentinians live in Buenos Aires. The city has a colorful culture. Its La Boca neighborhood has brightly painted houses. Artists sell their work at outdoor fairs. Local dancers perform on the sidewalks.

WHERE IS ARGENTINA ON THE MAP? WHICH COUNTRIES DOES IT BORDER?

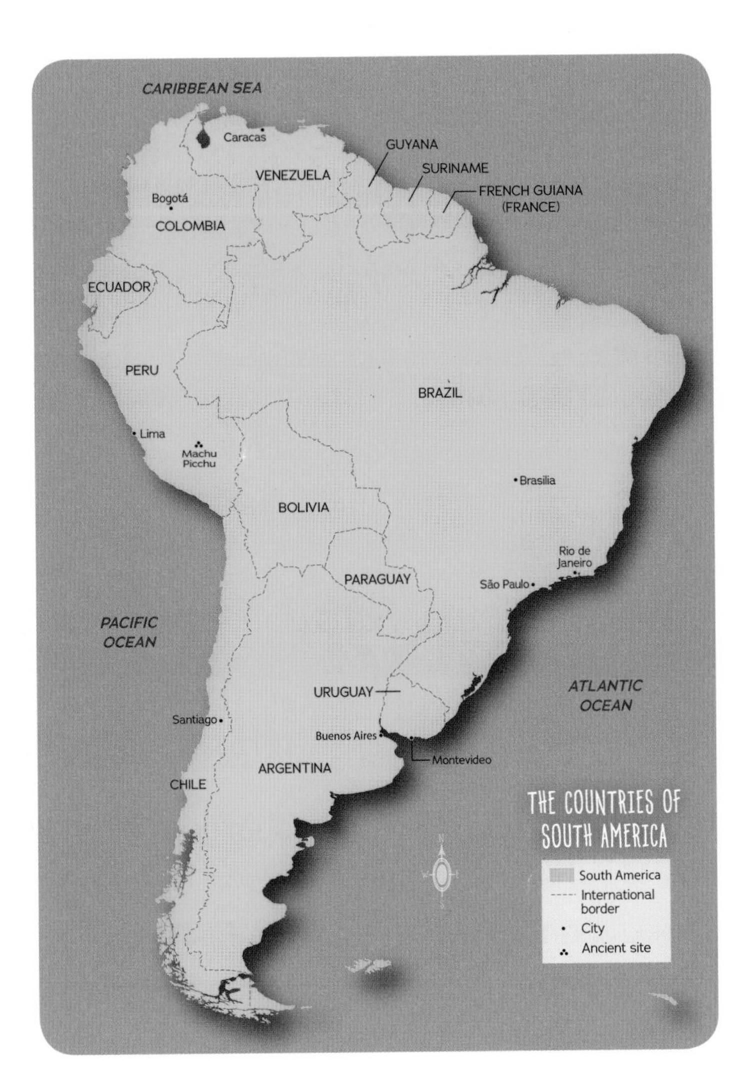

PERU HAS MANY POPULAR BEACHES.

Peru

Peru is another of South America's largest countries. It is a bit smaller than Alaska, the largest US state. Peru's capital, Lima, is on the Pacific coast. Fishing is a major industry for the city. Fishers catch sea bass and other fish along the coast.

The Incas and Machu Picchu

The Inca people were an indigenous group. They lived in what is now Peru. They built a city called Machu Picchu in the 1400s. It is high in the Andes Mountains. The Spanish took over the Incas' lands in the mid-1500s. In the 1900s, Machu Picchu became a popular tourist site.

Colombia

A third country with a large land area is Colombia. Colombia's western areas include part of the Andes Mountains. Its capital city, Bogotá, sits among these peaks. About seven million people live there. Bogotá has many universities. The city also has one of South America's oldest museums.

One of Bogotá's museums contains gold artifacts made by ancient indigenous people.

Chapter 3

LANDFORMS AND CLIMATE

South America's geography is diverse. It has many interesting landscapes. The continent has oceans, rain forests, deserts, and mountains.

South America is home to lush green forests and towering mountains. What other landscapes are found in South America?

People use traditional boats to travel on Lake Titicaca.

The Waters of South America

South America touches the Atlantic and Pacific Oceans. It borders the warm Caribbean Sea in the north. There are also important lakes. Lake Titicaca is one of the world's highest lakes. It sits at an elevation of 12,500 feet (3,800 meters). The lake borders Bolivia and Peru.

The world's highest waterfall is found on Venezuela's Churun River. Its name is Angel Falls. The waterfall drops 3,212 feet (979 m). The falls are located in a remote jungle. It is tough to reach them. Still, many tourists make the trip.

ANGEL FALLS IS NAMED FOR JIMMIE ANGEL. IN 1933, HE BECAME THE FIRST PILOT TO SEE THE WATERFALL FROM THE AIR.

The Amazon River lies mostly within Brazil, the continent's largest country. The Amazon is the world's second-longest river. Only the Nile River in Africa is longer.

The waters of the Amazon River make it possible for plants to grow. The region around the river is the Amazon rain forest. It is warm and rainy all year.

THE AMAZON RIVER TWISTS AND TURNS THROUGH NORTHERN SOUTH AMERICA.

Many types of plants thrive in the Amazon rain forest.

Deserts and Mountains

Not all of South America is as wet as its rain forests. The Atacama Desert lies southwest of the Amazon. It is one of the driest places on Earth. Few plants and animals can survive there.

AN AREA OF THE ATACAMA DESERT CALLED THE VALLEY OF THE MOON HAS DRAMATIC ROCKY LANDSCAPES.

The Pampas

The Pampas is a vast plain. It covers part of Argentina and most of Uruguay. It has two major areas. The western area is dry. The smaller eastern area is much wetter. The Pampas is known for its farms and ranches. Many of Argentina's large cities are there too.

The high peaks of the Andes are covered in snow.

The Andes Mountains lie east of the Atacama Desert. They begin near the continent's Caribbean coast. They stretch south for 5,500 miles (8,900 kilometers). Jagged peaks are found at South America's southern edge. Here, the weather can be very cold and windy.

WHICH CLIMATE ZONES ARE FOUND IN NORTHERN SOUTH AMERICA? WHICH ARE IN SOUTHERN SOUTH AMERICA? WHY MIGHT THEY DIFFER?

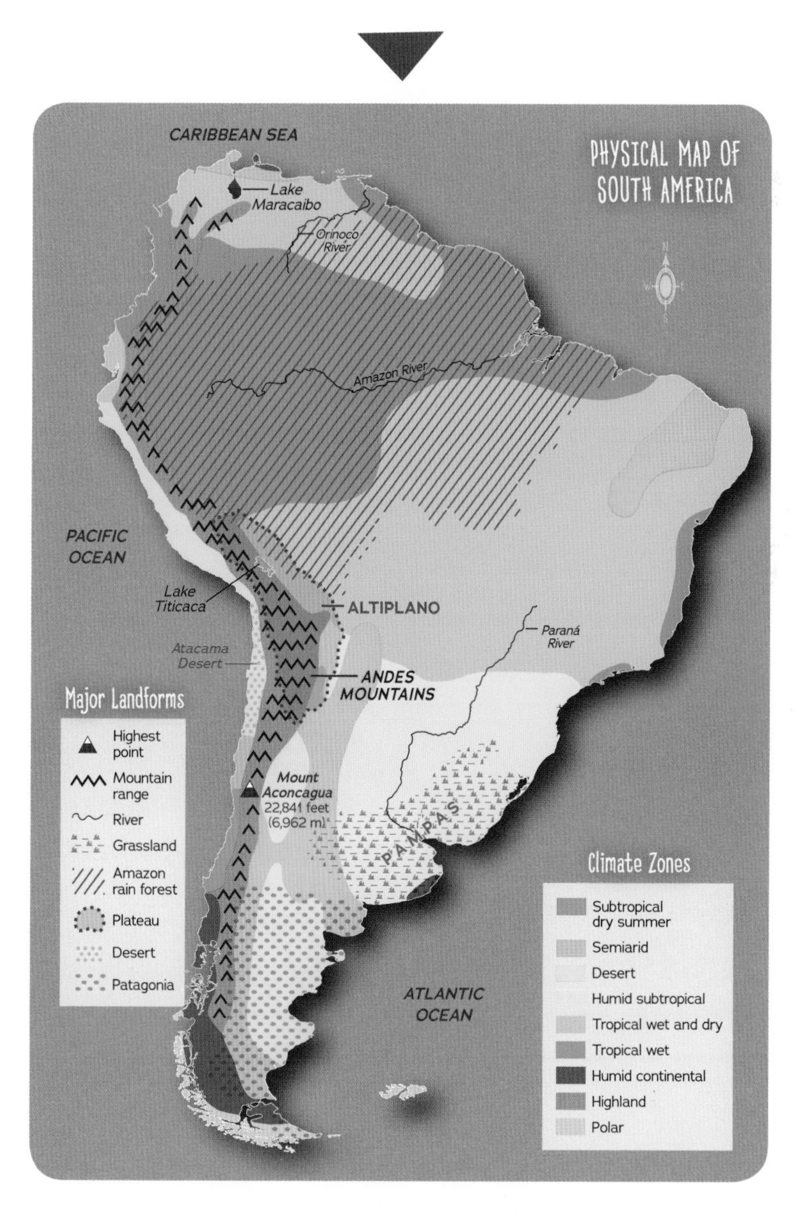

Chapter 4

NATURAL RESOURCES

South America has a wealth of natural resources. Crops grow well in its warm tropical areas. They also thrive in the Pampas. Diverse plants and animals live in the continent's rain forests.

Avocados are harvested in South America. Where in South America do crops grow?

Crops

Crops are important resources in South America. Avocado, pineapple, papaya, and guava grow there. Cacao and coffee are also major crops. Cacao beans are used to make chocolate. Cashews and Brazil nuts grow on tropical trees.

Animals

Many different animals live in South America's diverse landscapes. Cattle graze in the Pampas. Brazil, Uruguay, and Argentina produce beef. Sheep and alpacas live in colder areas. They have thick fur. This fur is made into fabric. It is sold around the world.

Alpaca fur has been used in clothing for thousands of years.

Life in the Amazon

The Amazon rain forest has a huge variety of animals. More than thirteen hundred types of birds live in the Amazon. This includes the colorful scarlet macaw. The forest's rivers have nearly three thousand species of fish. Among them is the arapaima. This huge fish measures up to 15 feet (4.6 m) long. Millions of insect species live in the Amazon too.

The scarlet macaw's colorful feathers help it blend in with the leaves, flowers, and fruits of the Amazon.

Deforestation

The Amazon rain forest has many kinds of trees. They include palm, rubber, and rosewood. People are overusing these natural resources. The wood is used as a building material. Farmers burn forests to clear space for crops and ranching. These activities harm animals and their habitats.

Chapter 5

PEOPLE AND CULTURES

South America is a mix of people from many cultures. Most South Americans have indigenous, European, and African ancestors. South Americans of indigenous and European ancestry are called mestizos.

These men are of indigenous descent. Where do most South Americans' ancestors come from?

Diversity

While mestizos make up a large part of South America's population, other groups live on the continent too. Many Japanese people live in Brazil. Middle Eastern immigrants live throughout the continent. People from Africa, Europe, and North America continue to move to South America.

Liberdade, a primarily Japanese neighborhood in São Paulo, Brazil, is popular among tourists.

Gauchos

Gauchos are similar to American cowboys. They worked as ranchers in the Pampas in the 1800s. They raised cattle and hunted wild horses. They are a symbol of pride in Argentina and Uruguay. They wore ponchos, baggy trousers, and wide-brimmed hats. Stories about gauchos are popular in the Pampas. Modern people sometimes dress as gauchos and put on shows.

CARNIVAL IS ONE OF THE WORLD'S BIGGEST PARTIES.

Carnival

The continent's diverse people celebrate many festivals. One of the biggest is Carnival. It mixes European and South American traditions. Carnival takes place all over South America. Performers wear colorful clothing. They dance in parades. A style of music and dance called samba is a big part of Carnival. Samba began in Brazil. It includes influences from Africa.

Chapter 6

ECONOMICS

South America has many important industries. Mining, energy, and tourism all make money for the continent's countries.

Mining is a key industry in South America. How else does the continent make money?

Mining

The Atacama Desert does not have many living things. But it does have copper. Chile produces more copper than any other country. Workers dig for it in deep mines. The copper is used in electronic products. Electric wires are made from copper.

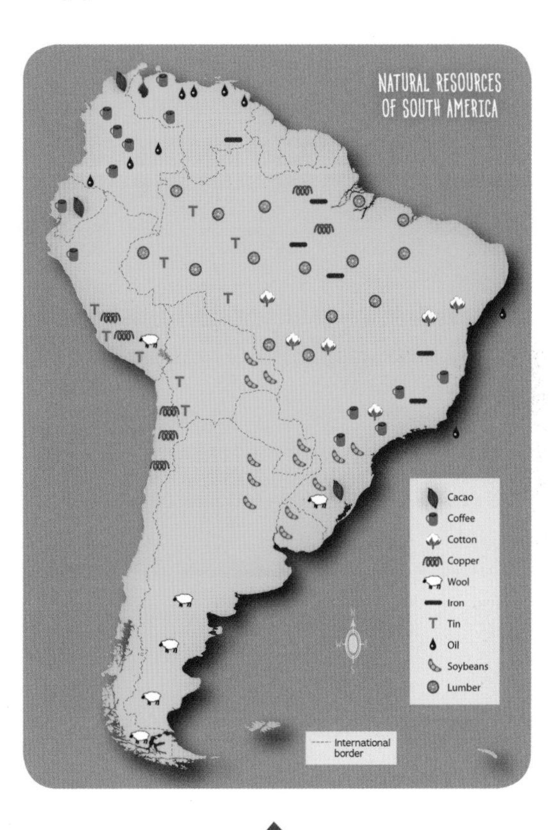

SPECIAL PUMPS ARE USED TO PULL OIL OUT OF THE GROUND.

Energy

Energy is an important resource. Venezuela produces oil. This fuel can power cars. It can be used to make electricity. Hydroelectric power plants use South America's rushing rivers. The water spins a turbine. This motion creates electricity. Water is the main source of power for South America.

Itaipú Dam

The Itaipú Dam is one of the world's largest hydroelectric power plants. It is located on the Paraná River. The dam is 5 miles (8 km) wide. It is on the border between Paraguay and Brazil. The power plant produces energy for both countries.

Tourism

South America is popular with tourists. People see historic sites, such as Machu Picchu. They travel to the rain forest to see amazing animals and plants. Tourists from all around the world come to see Carnival.

An Amazing Continent

South America is full of diverse people, cultures, and landscapes. You can find something new and exciting almost anywhere you look. Where will your South American adventure begin?

Incredible landscapes await visitors to South America.

Exploring South America

Choose two or three places from the map above that you want to know more about. Choose places from different parts of South America. Research these places online. What unique things are there to see and do? What do people eat? What festivals take place there? Write a paragraph about a trip that you will take to each place. What will you see and do?

Glossary

colony: a group of people who have left their country to settle in a new area

hydroelectric: using the power of moving water to spin turbines that produce electricity

immigrant: someone who moves from one country to live in another

indigenous: originally living in a particular area

poncho: a piece of woolen cloth worn as clothing

rain forest: a dense tropical forest that gets a lot of rain

species: a group of similar animals that are able to reproduce with one another

tropical: near Earth's equator

turbine: a wheel in a power plant that spins to create electricity

Learn More about South America

Books

Koponen, Libby. *South America.* New York: Children's Press, 2009. Learn about the landscapes and history of South America in this book.

Wojahn, Rebecca Hogue, and Donald Wojahn. *A Rain Forest Food Chain: A Who-Eats-What Adventure in South America.* Minneapolis: Lerner Publications, 2009. Learn about the diets of rain forest creatures and discover why every animal and plant in these habitats is important.

Woods, Mary B., and Michael Woods. *Seven Natural Wonders of Central and South America.* Minneapolis: Twenty-First Century Books, 2009. Explore a lake hidden in a volcano, the tallest waterfall in the world, and more of South America's greatest natural wonders.

Websites

How Stuff Works—What's Inside: South America
http://history.howstuffworks.com/south-american-history
Take a look at this site to learn more about South America's rich history.

Machu Picchu
http://www.history.com/topics/machu-picchu
Learn more about the construction of Machu Picchu and how the amazing site is being protected today.

Time for Kids: Argentina
http://www.timeforkids.com/destination/argentina
See photos of Argentina, discover a day in the life of Argentinian kids, and learn a few Spanish words and phrases.

Index

Photo Acknowledgments

The images in this book are used with the permission of: © Johan Sjolander/iStockphoto, p. 4; © Ammit Jack/Shutterstock Images, p. 5; © Laura Westlund/Independent Picture Service, pp. 6, 11, 23, 33, 37; © Rich Vintage/iStockphoto, p. 7; © Joesboy/iStockphoto, p. 8; © SuperStock/Glow Images, p. 9; © elxeneize/Shutterstock Images, p. 10; © Klaus Ulrich Mueller/Shutterstock Images, p. 12; © Davor Lovincic/iStockphoto, pp. 13, 20; © Free Wind 2014/Shutterstock Images, p. 14; © Steve Geer/iStockphoto, p. 15; © Vadim Petrakov/Shutterstock Images, p. 16; © Alice Nerr/iStockphoto, p. 17; © Anton Ivanov/Shutterstock Images, p. 18; © Atelopus/iStockphoto, p. 19; © Toni Flap/iStockphoto, p. 21; © cristiani/iStockphoto, p. 22; © Agenturfotograf/iStockphoto, p. 24; © powerofforever/iStockphoto, p. 25; © ThePalmer/iStockphoto, p. 26; © Pedarilhos/iStockphoto, p. 27; © hadynyah/iStockphoto, p. 28; © T photography/Shutterstock Images, p. 29; © sunsinger/Shutterstock Images, p. 30; © mmeee/iStockphoto, p. 31; © robas/iStockphoto, p. 32; © Fabio Filzi/iStockphoto, p. 34; © Nicolas deCorte/iStockphoto, p. 35; © Carlos Lijo/iStockphoto, p. 36.

Cover image: © Planet Observer/Universal Images Group via Getty Images.

Main body text set in Adrianna Regular 14/20.
Typeface provided by Chank.